LOVE SONNETS OF THE RENAISSANCE

LOVE SONNETS OF THE RENAISSANCE

Translated from
Italian, French, Spanish
and Portuguese
by
LAURENCE KITCHIN

FOREST BOOKS
LONDON ☆ 1990 ☆ BOSTON

PUBLISHED BY
FOREST BOOKS
20 Forest View, Chingford, London E4 7AY, U.K.
P.O. Box 438, Wayland, MA 01788, U.S.A.

First published 1990

Typeset in Great Britain by Cover to Cover, Cambridge
Printed in Great Britain by B.P.C.C. Wheatons Ltd, Exeter

British Library Cataloguing in Publication Data:
Love sonnets of the Renaissance: (Italian, French & Spanish)
1. Sonnets in European languages — Anthologies
I. Kitchin, Laurence
808.81'42

ISBN 0–948259–60–4

Library of Congress Catalogue Card No.
89–83343

Contents

To my wife, Hilary

Professor Laurence Kitchin, born in Bradford, was educated at Bootham School, York, and King's College, London. For several years he taught at Stanford, California, and at the City University of New York. An interest in Italian literature inherited from his father was reinforced by war service there. Recently he has contributed a series of articles on Renaissance subjects to the *Times Higher Education Supplement*. Many of the translations included here were broadcast by the B.B.C. on two separate occasions, along with the originals.

Preface

The majority of these translations, including the extract from *Il Cortegiano*, were commissioned by the B.B.C. Seven of the Petrarch sonnet versions appeared in *Il Confronto Letteraria*, No 4, 1985. The editions I have used are those of Neri, F., et al, Milano–Napoli, 1951; Cohen, G., Paris, 1950; Rivers, E.L., Columbus, 1964; and the Oxford Books of French and Portuguese Verse.

I am indebted to Hallam Tennyson, Professor Bernado Gicovate, Professor Lawrence Ryan and Professor Arthur Terry for invaluable encouragement: to my sister Lucy Kitchin for support, Miss Margaret and Miss Audrey Rolfe for expert secretarial assistance; and to my wife, who embodies the qualities displayed at Urbino, for her support.

Laurence Kitchin, 1990

Introduction

More often than not the Petrarchan sonnet, as met with by students in higher education, is a write-off where continuing interest in later life is concerned. Right up to Auden and Neruda the fourteen-liner has been tenaciously alive, an international currency; so why this indifference to the founding fathers in Italy, France, England and Spain, not to mention Portugal, and to the work in the sixteenth century of Petrarch's most distinguished followers? There are a number of reasons for the neglect. To begin with, far too many sonnets were produced. It follows that most of them are feeble imitations of the master's work, lacking the initial impulse and aping his mannerisms. This in turn has led to a concentration by literary historians on the quantitative aspect, on Petrarchism and the 'Petrarchan', on a concept of 'influence' tending to by-pass the detailed and concrete achievements of the poet, which don't get the attention given to Marvell or Donne by today's leading critics. And the Italian language is surprisingly inaccessible now. According to a survey of American colleges in 1974, more students were learning Russian than Italian and ten times more were learning Spanish. Add to this, a dismissal of Petrarch by the Italophile legislator Ezra Pound and the fact that, unlike Dante's epic, the sonnets are short on narrative and 'ideas', and you have gone far enough to account for the downgrading by default of a very great poet.

His love sonnets are centered on one woman, first seen in the church of St. Clare at Avignon on April 6th, 1327, as one of the poems reports. Another supplies the date of her death in 1348, also at Avignon, also on April 6th. Not only this precise information for the archives, but even the name given to the other half of one of the most crucial relationships in the history of literature is typical of an arrogance which can annoy some readers. In calling her Laura, meaning 'laurel' in Italian, he in fact gives her the status of consort to a prize-winning poet. He had already been publicly awarded a laurel wreath, earlier in his career than would have been possible without influential contacts. This revival of the ancient Roman custom may seem to be no more than an example of aristocratic pedantry. In Petrarch's case, however, results have justified the assumption that his poems would do honour to Laura as well as himself. Certainly she is very much alive in the sonnets which he pretended to regard as 'fragments' because they were not in Latin, after six hundred years.

But who was Laura and what were her relations with the poet? Her identity remains unknown, with Laurette de Noves a leading candidate. As to the second problem, we can be sure of one thing at least: Laura was not the dream girl of a celibate recluse. Petrarch fathered two illegitimate children, neither of them hers, and the first sonnet in this selection rings the changes on various symptoms of unfulfilled desire. For this condition the last line reproaches her explicitly. It would therefore be a big mistake to distance and freeze the Laura sequence in such concepts as neo-Platonism and Courtly Love. Both have a part in it, but their axis remains a real woman, known intimately at some undetermined distance short of actual seduction. The interplay gives rise to a vast range of moods involving emotion, intellect and what used to be called the soul, but Laura, for most if not all of the time, is a distillation of sex. And any lingering doubts as to her physical reality are dispelled by the poet's reaction to her death. There we have the direct expression of personal grief, on a level with Lear's mourning of Cordelia, informing the silvery lines. After the convincing visions of Laura in paradise, there is a startling burst of realism where Petrarch's self-analysis goes far enough to question the value of the whole experience. Was it worth the trouble?

The Laura sequence, then, is not only a landmark in the development of lyrical intimacy in European literature but a repository of psychological truth. At times, indeed, the modernity of attitude comes as a surprise and the poet's voice bears little relation to the two-dimensional father of conventions, mannerisms and 'influence' referred to in textbooks. What a Petrarch visualized only in general terms can never convey is the immediacy of these poems, the impact for example of the footprint or the banking up of emotion behind a reference to the exact time of Laura's death. We must, all the same, begin by recognizing the form within which this extraordinary range of effects is gained. Essentially the Petrarchan sonnet is built in two structural blocks: the first eight lines (octave) and the last six lines (sestet). The octave describes a mood and/or situation; the sestet resolves it, or at any rate alters the focus.

What does Petrarch do within this apparently simple and constricted little formula? Almost anyone can learn its rules, as a thousand imitations prove, and present-day teachers have obtained accurate exercises of them during routine course work by students who would never claim to be poets. Petrarch begins with the advantage, boldly preferred for this purpose over contemporary humanist Latin, of the Italian language, with its vowel sounds well adapted to rhyming and its musicality, now more or less familiar to everyone by way of grand opera. His fiction, like Shakespeare's, is much of the time briskly in touch with common speech, the small change of relaxed conversation such as you hear even today, but without vulgarisms. When Petrarch uses long words – 'egaulmente', 'mormorando' – they indicate a continuing process of mood or sound without interrupting the forward movement, the mellifluous rhythm. This is what singers call *legato*, and in sustaining it Petrarch has never been surpassed by any lyric poet. When actors read the sonnets aloud they are often in danger of destroying the *legato* by inserting dramatic emphasis, whereas the poems have an inward, brooding quality which corresponds to their musical flow, itself a product of the Italian language and this master's infallible ear for it.

Sometimes Petrarch will carry right through the octave with a single sentence. Sometimes there will be dialogue and dramatic tension, held in the movement and never histrionic or obtrusive. What can seem at first glance to be repetitively poised and elegant is in fact varied by every service in a lyric poet's armoury: changes of tone and tempo, underpinned by subtle rhyming and assonance. The last half of a sestet may be a monumental achievement of balance, and the weight of an inverted pyramid may bear on the very last line. These remain technicalities, not enough of course to account for the personal feeling transmitted. The essence of interplay in these poems between Petrarch and Laura is his unremitting dedication. But dedication to what? To a real woman he outlived and never slept with? More likely to 'Laura', perceived in the end as an embodiment of the transience and unpredictability of life itself.

Petrarch died in 1374; and, considered in terms of a lifetime of influential scholarship his sonnets were a sideline, not even written in Latin. His greatest follower in the form he had perfected was Ronsard (1524–1585), who described himself, until he found a voice of his own, explicitly as *petrarquisant*. He headed the Pléiade, a group of young men determined to exploit the legacy of Greece and Rome while composing in current French. They embodied the Renaissance in exuberant, self-confident vigour. Aside, however, from his revolutionary importance not only in French literature but as a model for the English Elizabethans, Ronsard is one of the world's great poets in his own right, and one of the world's great erotic poets at that. Yet he is chiefly known today as the author of a single admittedly great sonnet. How could such a thing come about? The first and obvious reason is Shakespeare, not superior as a sonneteer and with a very much smaller output, but favoured by preeminence in drama. A second, perhaps, may be the timeless appeal in French of Racine as a psychologist and of Baudelaire as the laureate of urban decay. But what gets most in the way of our enjoyment of Ronsard is his neoclassical furniture, the names and allusions inherited from the ancients. They abound in his verse, but so does an agile directress. All the same a phrase like 'ombres myrteux' asks for spontaneous recall of Latin verse if its effect is to be more than botanical. And we know what has happened to Latin as a university subject.

As between Petrarch and Ronsard a greater contrast in temperaments can scarcely be imagined. Subsidized as a minor cleric in holy orders attached to the court, Ronsard was equally at home in aristocratic circles and his country estates, where food, wine and the lure of peasant girls inform his poetry with an atmosphere like that of Jean Renoir's films. He enjoys making love, he announces. He enjoys talking to women, writing about his affairs; he delights in balls, dancing, masques, music and the lute, those enemies of care. Now he is in love with a brunette, now with a blonde. Since all this is carried through openly into his poetry, it sets him apart from the metaphysical halo conferred on Laura by his original model. For one thing Ronsard writes entire sonnet sequences to historically identifiable women: Cassandre, Marie, Hélène and others. For another, his blatant heterosexuality can lead to symptoms of frustration, described with uninhibited frankness or to a physical disgust on a par with Shakespeare's. This outgoing realism is in abeyance a lot of the time, for Ronsard can play tunes on the conventional instruments of neo-classicism or courtly love with the best of them. But we can tolerate the uneveness of a too prolific output because of his irrepressible, inexhaustible reserves of vitality.

So much for the man. Combine his personality with an early addiction to Homer and Virgil, substitute French for Petrarch's Italian, and interesting things happen to the sonnet. There will not be the *legato* obtainable from Italian vowels. Instead we have the French sound, crisper, probing and immediate. Not to recall variations within the fourteen-liner already drawn attention to in Petrarch, we can point out two major weapons of lyric poetry conspicuous in Ronsard as well: tempo and tone. When Petrarch is pacing deserted fields the verse movement is slow. In addressing the river Rhone on its way down to Laura's valley, he accelerates on the very first word of the sonnet's first line. With Ronsard there is a similar contrast between two of the poems included here (all six are in his original spelling). One begins with a four-line string of long vowels, drawn out in tune with the desolate nocturnal frustration he describes. The second spits out a protest, 'Injuste Amour . . .' In both cases the tone alters later as he charts his emotions. Compared with Petrarch's tendency to a low profile, Ronsard often stands in the foreground, abrupt and impatient. (It says much for the sonnet's flexibility that it can assimilate both.) And although Ronsard's exuberance is unique, after his initial use of Petrarch as a springboard, a late appeal to the unresponsive Hélène boasts that his sonnets have made her as celebrated as Laura.

Only one member of the original Pléiade group equalled Ronsard in some of his sonnets. This was his respected friend and author of their revolutionary manifesto, Joachim du Bellay (1522–1560). Unlike the others in this collection, the two poems by du Bellay are in no way erotic. They illustrate supreme mastery of the form, but also a clash of loyalties arising from the application of French language to Italian Renaissance models. We come upon a similar conflict when the Italianizing process arrives in England. Du Bellay's distinction is to have expressed the grandeur of Rome definitively, without losing his own national identity. To spend four years in a headquarters of the ancient world and yet to be homesick for Anjou results in creative ferment, the exile's longing. Bitterly wrenching the pastoral mode, he can express himself in terms of a strayed lamb, just as Garcilaso once empathized with the distracted motions of a lost dog in a deserted valley.

Once, however, du Bellay found an exact 'objective correlative' for his divided loyalties, a sonnet which exactly conveys the mood of millions of exiles, especially soldiers on foreign service, before and since. Its tone replaces the dejected self-pity of the lamb comparison with objective poise; there is no stridency and the feeling is deeper. Since nothing has so far been said of imagery as a constituent of sonnets, this one may be taken as an example. It starts off with an inspired simile of two words only, invoking the associations sparked off by Ulysses, that archetypal exile and soldier who took ten years to get home from a war. After an allusion to Jason the ancient world gives way to du Bellay's recall not only of France but specifically of his native Anjou, of his village and more precisely of his own courtyard. The imagery is visual, tactile, and where it includes air quality may even extend to taste and smell. Rome surfaces briefly as architecture in the sestet only to emphasize his preference for local building material in his village. In fact the weight of the entire sonnet, as anyone lucky enough to have heard Jean Vilar read it will agree, comes to bear on two words: 'ardois fine.' Who else but du Bellay has managed to concentrate timeless poetry on the texture of slate?

The new Italianate forms were firmly planted in the Spanish language by Garcilaso de la Vega (1501–1536) and his friend Boscán. Garcilaso, a major poet who published nothing in his lifetime, is best known for eclogues surpassing Edmund Spenser; but he mastered the Petrarchan sonnet. Courtier, soldier on the personal bodyguard of Emperor Charles V, scholar and poet, Garcilaso came as near as anyone to embodying the total Renaissance man. The stimulus for his finest poetry was love of a Portuguese court lady, sustained in the context of his marriage and hers and beyond her death, which had the effect of fixing Isabel Freire at the root of Garcilaso's creative imagination, a controlling shadow. Never overtly mentioned, she is always there.

In addition to the elements already pointed out Petrarch, of course, bequeathed to his followers such recurring erotic themes as absence, despairing confusion, the beloved's presence in natural scenery and her elevation of an ideal beauty. A favourite subject of his neo-classical successors derives from Horace's 'Carpe diem', 'seize the day'; or to put it crudely 'sleep with me now, because age will hit you sooner than you expect, and then you won't be invited.' Probably the best known version is Marvell's 'To his Coy Mistress', with its shock tactics and modernities like 'instant fires.' But this theme recurs in the sonnet and is one indication of Garcilaso's particular flavour. Of Ronsard's two versions included here the first moves briskly with a springtime delicacy towards a magical line which darkens the tone and quickens the pace: 'le tems s'en va, le tems s'en va, Ma Dame.' The second visualizes Hélène inexorably as a grey-haired old woman, goes on to implicate the poet himself in the ageing process and signs off with a rather flat last line, the customary invitation enforced by an exclamation mark. In fact he has evoked mortality so well that seduction fades into the background.

In most of the sonnets on this theme it is the sestet, meditating on time's revenge, which bears the weight; and

Garcilaso's is no exception. What marks his as original is the description of a lady's hair, intricate in itself and inseparable from the interwoven clauses of the octave, eight lines of one sentence not yet complete. Add to this the deliberate gravity of the tone and you have a poetic reflection of the Spanish courtier, his elaborate etiquette, his melancholy, his moody stoical stance as Velasquez saw them. The sestet is chilly, literally on the snowline. And yet Garcilaso's presence as a fragile, disorientated personality in the sonnets, can seem closer to present-day readers than any other of these poets. Inside the Spanish grandee killed in battle at thirty-six is a very modern self-analyst inhabiting a waste land, prematurely aged and playing it cool.

The most famous book of the sixteenth-century, however, was in prose: *The Book of the Courtier* by Baldassarre Castiglione (1478–1529). And it was typical of Garcilaso's place in the Renaissance ferment that he provided the introduction to the first Spanish translation. After all, he embodied as near as anyone, the qualities laid down for an ideal courtier, whose counterpart was an ideal court lady, presented in Book III. There Castiglione stages a lively debate, including issues such as equality of the sexes, which are still relevant almost five hundred years later.

Laurence Kitchin

The Sonnets

Petrarch
Ronsard
Du Bellay
Garcilaso de la Vega
Camões

Petrarch

Sonetto XXV

Solo e pensoso i più deserti campi
vo misurando a passi tardi e lenti,
e gli occhi porto per fuggire intenti
ove vestigio uman la rena stampi.
Altro schermo non trovo che mi scampi
dal manifesto accorger de le genti,
perché negli atti d'allegrezza spenti
di fuor si legge com'io dentro avvampi;

si ch'io mi credo omai che monti e piagge
e fiumi e selve sappian di che tempre
sia la mia vita ch'è celata altrui.
Ma pur si aspre vie ne si selvagge
cercar non so, ch'Amor non venga sempre
ragionando con meco, et io con lui.

Petrarch

Through the most arid fields my walks are planned,
Thoughtful and slowly measuring my stride
I go; and watchful, so that I can hide
If a human foot is printed on the sand.
There is no other shield which can withstand
The knowing looks inflicted from outside,
Because, all joyful motions nullified,
My look spells out the soul's consuming brand;

And so it is that henceforth I'm aware
Mountains and woods and river banks can see
The life I lead, that's hidden from mankind;
Nor can I search out paths so rough and bare
That Love will not insist on joining me,
Inseparable companion of my mind.

Petrarch

Sonetto CCVIII

Rapido fiume, che d'alpestra vena
rodendo intorno, onde 'l tuo nome prendi,
notte e di meco disioso scendi
ov'Amor me, te sol natura mena,
vattene innanzi: il tuo corso non frena
né stanchezza né sonno, e pria che rendi
suo dritto al mar, fiso u' si mostri attendi
l'erba più verde e l'aria più serena.

Ivi è quel nostro vivo e dolce sole
ch'adorna e 'nfiora la tua riva manca;
forse, o che spero! el mio tardar le dole.
Basciale 'l piede o la man bella e bianca;
dille, e 'l basciar sie 'n vece di parole:
Lo spirto è pronto, ma la carne è stanca.

Petrarch

Impetuous river, which from alpine meads
Eroding in a word that fits your sound,
Flows day and night with me to lower ground
Where love myself and you an instinct leads,
Go on ahead, no weariness impedes
Your progress: then stare fixedly around
Before the sea distrains, till you have found
A place of calmer skies and greener reeds.

There is our living and delightful sun
Who makes of your left bank eternal May,
I dare to hope she grieves that I'm outrun.
Kiss her white hand and foot for me and say,
As if the kisses and my words are one:
'The soul flies on, the body falls away.'

Petrarch

Sonetto CXXXIV

Pace non trovo e non ò da far guerra,
e temo e spero, et ardo e son un ghiaccio,
e volo sopra 'l cielo e giaccio in terra,
e nulla stringo e tutto l' mondo abbraccio.
Tal m'à in pregion, che non m'apre né serra,
né per suo mi riten né scioglie il laccio,
e non m'ancide Amore e non mi sferra,
né mi vuol vivo né mi trae d'impaccio.

Veggio senza occhi e non ò lingua e grido,
e bramo di perir e cheggio aita,
et ò in odio me stesso ed amo altrui.
Pascomi di dolor, piangendo rido,
egualmente mi spiace morte e vita:
in questo stato son, Donna, per vui.

Petrarch

Peace have I none, no neither peace nor war,
I fear and hope, I am afire and freeze,
I climb the skies and grovel on the floor,
Embrace the world itself, but nothing seize.
Such is my prison that it neither frees nor binds,
Will neither hold me back nor liberate,
Love neither kills me nor an outlet finds,
Grants no reprieve, or end to the debate.

Tongueless I cry and without eyes I see,
Call for assistance though I long to die.
I loathe myself and love what's out of reach,
laughing through tears I feed on misery,
Death and a life on earth both pass me by:
This is the doctrine, Lady, that you teach.

Petrarch

Sonetto CLXIV

Or che 'l ciel e la terra e 'l vento tace,
e le fere e gli augelli il sonno affrena,
notte il carro stellato in giro mena,
e nel suo letto il mar senz' onda giace,
vegghio, penso, ardo, piango, e chi mi sface
sempre m' è inanzi per mia dolce pena:
guerra è 'l mio stato, d' ira e di duol piena.
e sol di lei pensando ho qualche pace.

Cosi sol d'una chiara fonte viva
move 'l doce e l'amaro ond' io mi pasco;
una man sola mi risana e punge;
e perché 'l mio martir non giunga a riva,
mille volte il dì moro e mille nasco:
tanto da la salute mia son lunge!

Petrarch

The sounds of earth, of sky, of wind, now cease,
The birds and animals by sleep are tied,
Night wheels the constellations on their ride,
Waveless the sea reclines without a crease.
I watch, think, burn, and weep. Who wrecks my peace
Always confronts me, torture mollified,
My state is war, anger and grief's high tide,
Only the thought of her brings some release.

Thus from a single clear and living spring
Flows my repast, with sweet and bitter filled,
A single hand both heals and runs me through;
Lest there be limits to my suffering,
A thousand times I'm born, a thousand killed:
So far off is the health which I once knew.

Petrarch

Sonetto CLXXVI

Per mezzi boschi inospiti e selvaggi
onde vanno a gran rischio uomini et arme,
vo securo io, ché non può spaventarme
altri che 'l Sol ch'à d'Amor vivo i raggi;
e vo cantando, o penser miei non saggi,
lei che 'l ciel non poria lontana farme,
ch'i' l'ò negli occhi, e veder seco parme
donne e donzelle, e sono abeti e faggi.

Parmi d'udirla, udendo i rami e l'òre
e le frondi, e gli augei lagnarsi, e l'acque
mormorando fuggir per l'erba verde.
Raro silenzio, un solitario orrore
d'ombrosa selva mai tanto mi piacque;
se non che dal mio Sol troppo si perde.

Petrarch

Deep in the wood's wild, uninviting ways
Where even men-at-arms must watch their tread
Immune I go, since all I have to dread
Is amorous burning, Love's own solar rays.
And I go singing, prey to foolish thoughts
Of her, who's near me under every sky,
Always in sight; To my deluded eye
Fir tree and birch are ladies, her escorts.

I seem to hear her, as I hear the sound
Of leaves, of branches, birds and trembling air,
Elusive water murmuring through the green.
Rarely have solitude and dangerous ground,
Arboreal darkness, so dispelled all care.
Only my Sun's not here; nor has she been.

Petrarch

Sonetto CXLIX

Qual paura ò quando mi torna a mente
quel giorno ch'i' lasciai grave e pensosa
Madonna, e 'l mio cor seco! non è cosa
che si volentier pensi e sì sovente.
I' la riveggio starsi umilemente
tra bell donne a guisa d'una rosa
tra minor fior; né lieta né dogliosa,
come chi teme ed altro mal non sente.

Deposta avea l'usata leggiadria,
le perle e le ghirlande e i panni allegri
e 'l riso e 'l canto e 'l parlar dolce umano.
Così in dubbio lasciai la vita mia:
or tristi auguri e sogni e penser negri
mi danno assalto, e piaccia a Dio che 'in vano.

Petrarch

Great is my fear when I recall to mind
My Lady on the day I saw her last.
Too well I see her pensive and downcast.
As I took leave, I left my heart behind.
Again I see her holding back, subdued
A rose among the beauties of the court,
Those lesser flowers; not happy or distraught,
Like one by fear, and fear alone, pursued.

She had renounced embellishments of dress,
Pearls, festive robes, and garlands for the hair,
Laughter and singing and her sweet converse.
My life itself I left behind, no less.
Now dismal omens, dreams and black despair
Crowd in on me: Please God, there comes no worse.

Petrarch

Sonetto CCCX

Zefiro torna e 'l bel tempo rimena,
e i fiori e l' erbe, sua dolce famiglia,
e garrir Progne e painger Filomena,
e primavera candida e vermiglia;
ridono i prati e 'l ciel si rasserena,
Giove s' allegra di mirar sua figlia,
l' aria e l' acqua e la terra è d' amor piena,
ogni animal d' amar si riconsiglia.

Ma per me, lasso, tornano i più gravi
sospiri, che del cor profondo tragge
quella ch' al ciel se ne portò le chiavi;
e cantar augelletti e fiorir piagge
e 'n belle donne oneste atti soavi
sono un deserto e fere aspre e selvagge.

Petrarch

Zefirus brings fine weather back again,
Flowers and new grass, his gentle family,
Procne to chide and Filomel complain;
White or vermilion spring is on each tree.
The meadows laugh, the sky is cleared of rain,
Jove looks upon his progeny with glee,
Love is all air and water can contain
And every creature towards love roams free.

To me and my despair he brings no ease,
But sighs profoundly drawn from my heart strings
By her who wears its keys at heaven's feasts;
And singing birds, the hillside blossomings,
The actions by which lovely women please,
Is wilderness, the haunt of savage beasts.

Petrarch

Sonetto CCCXXVI

Tornami a mente, anzi v'è dentro, quella
ch'indi per Lete esser non pò sbandita,
qual io la vidi in su l'età fiorita
tutta accesa de' raggi di sua stella;
si nel mio primo occorso onesta e bella
veggiola, in sé raccolta e sì romita,
ch'i grido: "Ell'è ben dessa, ancor è in vita",
e 'n don le cheggio sua dolce favella.

Talor risponde e talor non fa motto;
i', come uom ch'erra e poi più dritto estima,
dico a la mente mia: "Tu se' 'ngannata:
sai che 'n mille trecento quarant otto,
il dì sesto d'aprile, in l'ora prima,
del corpo uscìo quell'anima beata".

Petrarch

Back to my mind she comes, deep rooted there,
Whom even Lethe never can displace
As I beheld her in her vernal grace
Ablaze with her own star's heavenly glare.
Just as at our first meeting, chastely fair,
So self-contained, so perfectly in place
That I cry 'This is her yet living face',
And ask to hear that voice beyond compare.

Sometimes she answers, sometimes she will wait;
I, like one steadied by his reason's power,
Say to my mind, "Your judgment is astray.
You know in thirteen hundred forty-eight,
On the sixty day of April, its first hour,
From the body that blest spirit stole away."

Petrarch

Sonetto CCCXLVI

Li angeli eletti e l'anime beate
cittadine del cielo, il primo giorno
che Madonna passò, le fur intorno
piene di meraviglia e di pietate.
"Che luce è questa e qual nova beltate"
dicean tra lor "per ch'abito sì adorno
dal mondo errante a qest'alto soggiorno
non salì mai in tutta questa etate?"

Ella, contenta aver cangiato albergo,
si paragona pur coi più perfetti,
e parte ad or ad or si volge a tergo
mirando s'io la seguo, e par ch'aspetti:
ond'io voglie e pensier tutti al ciel ergo,
perch'i l'odo pregar pur ch'i'm'affretti.

Petrarch

Blest souls and loyal angels in their might,
Heaven's citizens, assembled on the way
My Lady walked among them that first day,
Filled with respect and marvelling delight.
"What unknown beauty is this, and what light?"
They said, "for never one in such array
In all the ages has been seen to stray
From the sinful world to this exalted height."

She, happy to be lodged with her own kind
And perfect as the best who pass the gate,
Turns back repeatedly, as if to find
If I am following, and seems to wait:
My thoughts and wishes fly there unconfined;
She is impatient because I am late.

Petrarch

Sonetto CCCXX

Sento l'aura mia antica, e i dolci colli
veggio apparire onde 'l bel lume nacque,
che tenne gli occhi miei mentr'al ciel piacque
bramosi e lieti, or li ten tristi e molli.
O caduche speranze, o penser folli!
Vedove l'erbe e torbide son l'acque,
e voto e freddo 'l nido in ch'ella giacque,
nel qual io vivo e morto giacer volli,

sperando alfin da le soavi piante
e da' belli occhi suoi che 'l cor m'ànn'arso
riposo alcun de le fatiche tante.
Ò servito a signor crudele e scarso:
ch'arsi quanto 'l mio foco ebbi davante,
or vo piagendo il suo cenere sparso.

Petrarch

I breathe remembered air, calm hills again
Where my own star was born come into sight,
Which kept my eyes, while heaven gave that right,
Eager and glad, and bathes them now with pain.
Decaying hopes and reasoning insane!
Bereft the grass, turbid the water's flight,
Empty and cold her nest upon this height,
Where I survive and rather dead had lain.

Hoping from her soft footstep at the last,
From eyes which seared my heart with beauty's ray,
Some respite from so many labours past.
I served a cruel lord for meagre pay:
I burned when my own fire was blazing fast,
Now I lament the embers turning grey.

Ronsard

Continuation des Amours, XXXV

Je vous envoye un bouquet que ma main
Vient de trier de ces fleurs epanies:
Qui ne les eust a ce vespre cuillies,
Flaques a terre elles cherroient demain.
Cela vous soit un exemple certain
Que voz beautés, bien qu'elles soient fleuries,
En peu de temps cherront toutes fletries,
Et periront, comme ces fleurs, soudain.

Le tems s'en va, le tems s'en va, ma Dame,
Las! le tems, non, mais nous, nous en allons,
Et tost serons estendus sous la lame:
Et des amours desquelles nous parlons,
Quand serons morts, n'en sera plus nouvelle:
Pour ce, aimés-moi, ce pendant qu'estes belle.

Ronsard

I send, by my own hands gathered and bound,
These opening flowers entwined in a bouquet:
Had no one picked them at the close of day,
Tomorrow they'd be sprinkled on the ground.
By their example you may surely know
That your own loveliness, now in its prime,
Itself will wither in as brief a time,
Drop like these flowers and perish at a blow.

Time hurries on, my lady, hurries on:
Alas, not time, ourselves are on our way,
And soon beneath the scythe we will be gone:
And intimacies we discuss today,
When we are dead they too will cease to be.
While you are beautiful, therefore, love me.

Ronsard

Amours de Cassandre, XXVIII

Injuste Amour, fusil de toute rage
Que peut un coeur soumis a ton pouvoir,
Quand il te plaist par les sens esmouvoir
Nostre raison qui preside au courage?
Je ne voy pré, fleur, antre ny rivage,
Champ, roc ny bois ny flots dedans le Loir,
Que peinte en eux, il ne me semble voir
Cette beauté qui me tient en servage.

Ores en forme ou d'un foudre allumé,
Ou d'un torrent, ou d'un tigre affamé,
Par fantaisie Amour de nuict les guide.
Mais quand ma main en songe les poursuit,
Le feu, la nef, et le torrent me fuit,
Et pour le vray je ne pren que le vuide.

Ronsard

Love the unjust, incendiary of rage,
What frees the heart subjected to your might
When you decide the senses will incite
Reason itself to halt and disengage?
No meadow, flower or hidden anchorage,
No wavelet on the Loir or rocky height,
But painted on them I believe I sight
This beauty holding me in vassalage.

Now in the form of thunderbolt aflame,
Of torrent, or of tiger scenting game,
Love guides nocturnal fantasies towards me.
But when in dreams my hand is raised to strike,
Trail, fire and torrent vanish all alike,
Instead of prey I grasp vacuity.

Ronsard

Sonnets pour Hélène, 2, XLII

Ces longues nuicts d'hyver, où la Lune ocieuse
Tourne si lentement son char tout à l'entour,
Où le coq si tardif nous annonce le jour,
Où la nuict semble un an a l'ame soucieuse:
Je fusse mort d'ennuy sans ta forme douteuse
Qui vient par une feinte alleger mon amour
Et, faisant toute nue entre mes bras sejour,
Me pipe doucement d'une joye menteuse.

Vraye, tu es farouche, et fiere en cruauté:
De toi fausse on jouist en toute privauté,
Pres ton mort je m'endors, pres de luy je repose,
Rien ne m'est refusé. Le bon sommeil ainsi
Abuse par le faux mon amoureux souci.
S'abuser en amour n'est pas mauvaise chose.

Ronsard

Through these long winter nights the slow moon wheels
In lazy arcs on its extended way,
So very late the cock announces day,
And in my soul a year-long night unreels.
I'd die; but that my fantasy reveals
Your form, come here its passion to allay;
Entirely naked in my arms you stay:
A lying joy, with spurious appeals.

The real you is heartless, proud and crude;
The false can be enjoyed in solitude:
Your phantom shares my bed and you submit;
To ask for is to have. So sleep is kind,
Calming with falsity my amorous mind.
There are worse things in love than faking it.

Ronsard

Meslanges, 2, VI

Quand je suis tout bessé sur votre belle face,
Je vois dedans vos yeux je ne sçay quoy de blanc,
Je ne sçay quoy de noir, qui m'esmeut tout le sang.
Et qui jusques au cueur de veine en veine passe.
Je voy dedans Amour, qui va changeant de place,
Ores bas, ores haut, tousjours me regardant,
Et son arc contre moi coup sur coup debandant.
Las! Si je faux, raison, que veux-tu que j'y face?

Tant s'en faut que je sois alors maitre de mo.
Que je vendrois mon pere, et trahirais mon Roi,
Mon pais, et ma soeur, mes freres et ma mere.
Tant je suis hors du sens apres que j'a taté
A longs traits amoureux de la poison amere
Qui sort de ces beaux yeux dont je suis enchanté!

Ronsard

When I lie prone above your lovely face
Your eyes reveal strange glints of white, of black,
And my whole bloodstream seethes along its track
Right to the heart itself the colours race.
What they disclose is Love, who changes place,
Now low, now high, bow bent and staring back.
Shot after shot I suffer his attack.
Reason, if I'm deluded, state your case!

Such loss of self-control these visions bring
I would betray my father and my king,
My sisters, brothers, mother — yes, and France.
So crazed I am, having drunk long and well
A venom spurted by our dalliance
Out of the eyes which hold me in their spell.

Ronsard

Sonnets pour Hélène, 2, XLIII

Quand vous serez bien vieille, au soir a la chandelle,
Assise aupres du feu, devidant et filant,
Direz chantant mes vers, en vous esmerveillant:
Ronsard me celebroit du temps que j'estois belle.
Lors vous n'aurez servante oyant telle nouvelle,
Desja sous le labeur a demy sommeillant,
Qui au bruit de mon nom ne s'aille resveillant,
Benissant vostre nom, de louange immortelle.

Je seray sous la terre, et fantôme sans os
Par les ombres myrteux je prendray mon repos;
Vous serez au fouyer une vieille accroupie,
Regrettant mon amour et vostre fier desdain.
Vivez, si m'en croyez, n'attendez a demain:
Cueillez dés aujordhuy les roses de la vie.

Ronsard

When you are old, by evening candlelight
At the fireside spinning your time away,
Marvelling you'll intone my verse and say:
"Ronsard praised me, my beauty was so bright."
Then, at this proof of deathless fame you cite,
Though working half-asleep by end of day,
Your women at the sound of Ronsard's lay
Will waken one and all and sit upright.

I will be underground. Boneless with those
Ghosts in the shade of myrtle I'll repose;
You by the hearth a stooping old housewife,
Regretting my love and your proud disdain.
I urge you, live! Forestall tomorrow's pain,
Gather today the roses of your life.

Du Bellay

Les Regrets XXXI

Heureux qui, comme Ulysse, a fait un beau voyage,
Ou comme cestuy là qui conquit la toison,
Et puis est retourné, plein d'usage & raison,
Vivre entre ses parents le reste de son aage!
Quand revoiray-je, helas, de mon petit village
Fumer la cheminee, & en quelle saison
Revoiray-je le clos de ma pauvre maison,
Qui m'est une province, & beaucoup d'avantage?

Plus me plaist le sejour qu'ont basty mes ayeux,
Que des palais Romains le front audacieux:
Plus que le marbre dur me plaist l'ardoise fine.
Plus mon Loyre Gualois que le Tybre latin,
Plus mon petit Lyré que le mont Palatin,
Et plus que l'air marin la doulceur Angevine.

Du Bellay

Happy the man, back with a well stocked mind,
Who, like Ulysses, last voyage charted clear,
Or Jason and his golden souvenir,
Can live out his last years with his own kind!
Alas, when shall I see the smoke unwind
From my small village? At what time of year will
My poor country courtyard reappear,
To me a province, and much more, I find?

More to my taste the house my fathers made
Than some proud Roman's arrogant facade:
More than hard stone I like the fine grained slate,
More my French Loire than Tiber's Latin vine,
More my minute Lyré than Palatine.
More than sea air, Anjou I celebrate.

Du Bellay

Les Regrets IX

France, mère des arts, des armes et des loix,
Tu m'as nourry long temps du laict de ta mamelle:
Ores, comme un aigneau qui sa nourrisse appelle,
Je remplis de ton nom les antres et les bois.
Si tu m'as pour enfant advoue quelquefois,
Que ne me respons-tu maintenant, o cruelle?
France, France, respons a ma triste querelle.
Mais nul, sinon Echo, ne respond a ma voix.

Entre les loups cruels, j'erre parmy la plaine,
Je sens venir l'hyver, de qui la froide haleine
D'une tremblante horreur fait herisser ma peau.
Las, tes autres aigneaux n'ont faute de pasture,
Ils ne craignent le loup, le vent ny la froidure:
Si ne suis-je pourtant le pire du troppeau.

Du Bellay

Mother of arts, law, military fame,
France, for a long time you would suckle me:
Now, like a lamb fretting his nurse to see,
I fill the woods and caverns with your name.
Having at times acknowledged whence I came,
Why do you answer so reluctantly?
France, cruel France, answer my dismal plea:
Nothing but Echo answers me again.

Wolves as I search the plain could be my death,
I feel the winter coming with cold breath
And my skin bristles, trembling from the shock.
Your other lambs, well fed and near the fold,
Are not in fear of wolf, of wind, of cold.
Yet I am not the worst of all the flock.

Garcilaso de la Vega

Soneto XVII

Pensando qu'el camino iba derecho,
vine a parar en tanta desventura
que imaginar no puedo, aun con locura,
algo de que esté un rato satisfecho:
el ancho campo me parece estrecho,
la noche clara para mí es escura,
la dulce compania amarga y dura,
y duro campo de batalla el lecho.

Del sueño, si hay alguno, aquella parte
sola que es ser imagen de la muerte
se aviene con el alma fatigada.
En fin que, como quiera, 'stoy de arte
que juzgo ya por hora menos fuerte,
aunque en ella me vi, la que es pasada.

Garcilaso de la Vega

I thought the road I walked went straight ahead
But such a misadventure halted me
I can't imagine, even distractedly,
the slightest hint of a safe path to tread.
The whole broad countryside appears a thread,
The night is clear that I no longer see,
Bitter and hard is all sweet company
And a hard field of battle is the bed.

Of sleep, if any comes, only that part
Where death's imagined lineaments are found
Confronts the worn out spirit's inward eye.
It ends in this: The limit of my art
Is that I recognize as less profound,
However bad it was, the pain gone by.

Garcilaso de la Vega

Soneto XXIII

En tanto que de rosa y azucena
se muestra la color en vuestro gesto
y que vuestro mirar ardiente, honesto,
enciende el corazon, y lo refrena;
y en tanto que el cabello, que en la vena
del oro se escogió, con vuelo presto,
por el hermoso cuello blanco, enhiesto,
el viento mueve, esparce y desordena;

coged de vuestra alegre primavera
el dulce fruto, antes que el tiempo ayrado
cubra de nieve la hermosa cumbre.
Marchitará la rosa el viento helado
todo lo mudará la edad ligera,
por no hazer mudanza en su costumbre.

Garcilaso de la Vega

Because the tints of lily and the rose
Reveal their colours in your countenance,
And your most decorous yet burning glance
Inflames the heart while bidding it repose;
Because your hair, which sinuously glows,
Twined in its golden threads to crown the white
Incomparable neck, a random flight
Of breezes can unloose and discompose;

Now in your vernal joy store up a wealth
Of luscious fruit, before outrageous time
Covers the lovely summit deep in snow.
The rose will wither under windblown rime,
All will be changed as age comes on by stealth.
He will make no exceptions, you should know.

Garcilaso de la Vega

Soneto XXXIV

Gracias al cielo doy que ya del cuello
del todo el grave yugo he desasido,
y que del viento el mar embravecido
veré desde la tierra sin temello.
Veré colgada de un sutil cabello
la vida del amante embebecido
en su error, y en su engaño adormecido,
sordo a las voces que le evisan dello.

Alegraráme el mal de los martales;
mas no es mi corazon tan inhumano
en aqueste mi error come parece,
porque yo hulgo, come huelga al sano,
no de ver a los otros en los males,
sino de ver que dellos él carece.

Garcilaso de la Vega

I thank my stars that I have broken loose
From the heavy yoke that once constricted me
And that the windswept anger of the sea
I'll watch from dry land, having made a truce.
I'll watch, suspended from its slender noose,
The lover's life, enchanted by a hair,
Lulled by illusion, drowning in error there,
Deaf to advice, enjoying her abuse.

Human misfortunes will be my relief.
Not that I banish them from my own soul
Or am dehumanized, as it might seem.
I will rejoice like one who is made whole,
Not at the sight of others come to grief;
Simply their pain dispelled his own bad dream.

Garcilaso de la Vega

Soneto XXXVIII

Estoy contino en lágrimas bañado,
Rompiendo siempre el aire con sospiros,
Y más me duele el non osar deciros
Que he llegado por vos a tal estado;
Que viéndome do estoy y en lo que he andado
Por el camin estrecho da seguiros,
Si me quiero tornar para hüiros,
Desmayo, viendo atrás lo que he dejado;

Y si quiero subir a l'alta cumbre,
A cada paso espántanme en la vía.
Ejemplos tristes de los que han caído;
Sobre todo, me falta ya la lumbre,
De la esperanza, con que andar solía
Por la oscura región de vuestro olvido.

Garcilaso de la Vega

With no respite I am in tears immersed,
Piercing the air with sighing through the day,
And worst of all is that I dare not say
It is because of you I am accursed,
That seeing where I am, the ground traversed
In following you along this narrow way,
If I turned back and fled in disarray,
I'd swoon to see the place where I was first.

And if I wish to climb the topmost height
At every step I recognize and fear
The dismal fall of others you reject.
The ultimate is failure of the light
Of hope, till now a partner with me here
In the obscure region which is your neglect.

Garcilaso de la Vega

Soneto XXXVII

A la entrada de un valle, en un desierto
Do nadie atravesaba ni se vía,
Vi que con estrañeza un can hacía
Estremos de dolor con desconcierto:
Ahora suelta el llanto al cielo abierto,
Ora va rastreando por la vía;
Camina, vuelva, para, y todavía
Quedaba desmayado como muerto.

Y fue que se apartó de su presencia
Su amo, y no le hallaba, y esto siente;
Mirad hasta dó llega el mal de ausencia.
Movióme a compasión ver su accidente;
Dijele, lastimado: "Ten paciencia,
Que yo alcanzo razón, y estoy ausente."

Garcilaso de la Vega

Where a valley opens and the soil is bare,
Traversed by none, no place for man to stray,
I saw the antics of a dog's dismay
In the extremity of his despair.
Now his howl reaches high into the air,
Now he skims back and forth with no delay,
He turns, he walks, he halts; and all the way
Like a dead thing he was collapsing there.

His master's presence taken from his side,
Not to be found, anxiety makes him run.
Look how by separation we are tried.
Watching in pity how he is undone,
I say to him: "Be patient. We're allied.
I, armed with reason, mourn an absent one."

Garcilaso de la Vega

Soneto XXVI

Echado está por tierra el fundamento
Que mi vivir cansado sostenía
Oh cuánto bien s'acaba en solo un día!
Oh cuántas esperanzas lleva el viento!
Oh cuán ocioso está mi pensamiento
Cuando se ocupa en bien de cosa mía!
A mi esperanza, así como a baldía,
Mil veces la castiga mi tormento.

Las más veces me entrego, otras resisto
Con tal furor, con una fuerza nueva,
Que un monte puesto encima rompería.
Aquéste es el deseo que me lleva
A que desee tornar a ver un día
A quien fuera mejor nunca haber visto.

Garcilaso de la Vega

Upon the earth is that foundation thrown
By which my weary being was sustained.
Oh, how much good in but a day is drained!
How many hopes along the wind are blown!
Where it concerns the benefits I own,
In what futility my thought's engrained!
A thousand times delusive hope's maintained,
There for my torment, barren land unsown.

Usually patient, sometimes I have been
Seized with such fury, such access of strength,
I could fragment a mountain piled above.
It is the impulse to return at length
One day, and to behold again the love
It had been better never to have seen.

Camões

O Frecheiro Cego

Esta o lascivo e doce passarinho
com o biquinho as penas ordenando,
o verso sem medida, alegre e brando
despedindo ne rustico raminho;
o cruel caçador, que de caminho
se vem calada e manso desviando
com pronta vista a seta endireitando
lhe dá no estigio layo eterno ninho.

Desta arte o coração, que libra andava
posto que ja de longe destinado,
onde menos temia foi ferido;
porque o frecheiro cego me esperava
para que me tomasse descuidado,
en vossos claros olhos escondido.

Camões

This gentle bird which frolics in the brake,
Its little beak on preening so intent,
Sings without pause, delightedly content,
But soon its rural branches will forsake.
The cruel hunter, senses all awake,
Quiet and stealthy as he leaves the road,
Takes aim with bow and arrow that forebode
A nest forever in the stygian lake.

Exactly so the heart, which wandered free,
And just as fate had long ago decreed,
Was caught off guard and wounded in the field;
For the blind archer lay in wait for me,
To ambush me when I took little heed.
In those clear eyes of yours he was concealed.

Ronsard

Continuation des Amours, LXV

Je veus lire en trois jours l'Iliade d'Homère
Et pur ce, Corydon, ferme bien l'huis sur moi
Si rien me vient troubler, je t'asseure ma foi,
Tu sentiras combien pesante est ma colere.
Je ne veus seulement que notre chambriere
Vienne faire mon lit, ou m'apprete de quoi
Je menge, car je veux demeurer à requoi
Trois jours, pour faire apres un an de bonne chere.

Mais si quelcun venait de la part de Cassandre,
Ouvre-luit tost la porte, et ne le fais attendre:
Soudain entre en ma chambre, et me viens accoustrer.
Je veux tanseulement a lui seul me monstrer;
Au reste si un Dieu voulait pour moi descendre
Due ciel, ferme la porte et ne le laisse entrer.

Ronsard

I'll read the Iliad in just three days;
So make sure, Corydon, you bar the door:
If I'm disturbed I promise, God before,
You'll find how heavily my anger weighs.
Instruct our chambermaid that she delays
To cook or make my bed for three days more.
I'll segregate myself in Homer's war
Meanwhile, and then a year of holidays.

But should Cassandra's messenger come here,
Open immediately, he must not wait;
Enter my room and deck me out in pride.
To him alone I'm anxious to appear.
Otherwise, if a god descends in state
To see me, close the door. He stays outside.

The Court Lady

(from *Il Cortegiano*)

Baldassarre Castiglione

Baldassarre Castiglione

The Court Lady

CASTIGLIONE: Alle pendici dell 'Appenino, quasi al mezzo della Italia verso il mare Adriatico, è posta, come ognun sa, la piccola città di Urbino . . .

On the slopes of the Appenines, almost in the centre of Italy on the Adriatic side, there stands (as everybody knows) the little city of Urbino, which — being sited in a mountainous region, and so lacking, perhaps, the amenities of many others to be found elsewhere — has nevertheless a climate favourable enough to ensure a highly fertile countryside, abounding with fruit. And so, in addition to the healthiness of the atmosphere, a most plentiful supply of everything necessary to sustain human life is to be found. The palace of Urbino, considered by many to be the finest in all Italy, was built for the Duca Federico, of glorious memory; and here, in the time of his son, the Duca Guidobaldo, I was present at those discussions upon which my 'Book of the Courtier' is based . . . Over them presided the Duchessa Elisabetta Gonzaga, assisted by the Signora Emilia Pia, and gentlemen of the most noble and valorous character took part . . .

BERNARDO: . . . there have been many other men who caused amusement in such a way; and indeed this behaviour is praiseworthy in men who have no other profession, but the Courtier's jokes ought to fall short a little of scurrility. One should also take care that practical jokes do not extend to fraud, for many evil men are to be observed who go about the world practising various deceptions to gain money feigning first one thing and then another. Jokes should not be too bitter, and above all, in this as in everything else, respect and courtesy should be maintained towards women, particularly where reflections on their chastity are in question.

Gasparo: Really, Messer Bernardo, you are too prejudiced in favour of these women. Now, why do you consider that men should deal more respectfully with women than with men? Does it seem to you that women may run men through with words and tricks on every occasion, without any restraint, and the men should bear it in silence, and show gratitude for being at a disadvantage?

Bernardo: I don't deny that women should maintain, both in verbal and practical jokes, the respect we have already spoken of towards men: what I do say is that they may be given wider scope in attacking men, on questions of chastity, than men may claim in attacking women; and this because we ourselves have made a rule that, in us, a dissolute life is no vice, deficiency or justification for slander at all, whereas in a woman it is so extreme an insult and shame that she who is once spoken badly of — whether the calumny laid upon her be true or false — will *always* be reproached. Therefore, since casting doubt on the honour of women is a thing sufficiently dangerous to harm them seriously, I say that we should attack them on other subjects and abstain from this; for if the witticism or practical joke strikes too severely, it exceeds the bounds which we have already said are fitting to a gentleman.

Ottaviano: Signor Gasparo might well reply to you, that this rule which you allege we ourselves have made is not perhaps as unreasonable as you think; for as women are the most imperfect of creatures, with little or no dignity in comparison to men, and are incapable of carrying out any virtuous action on their own account, it was necessary to harness them with shame and the fear of bad reputation and, as it were, forcibly to introduce some good qualities into them. And it would appear that continence, more than any other, was necessary for them, so as to safeguard their offspring. Hence it has been imperative by every art, means and contrivance to make women chaste, while giving them a free hand in everything else to be futile and always to do the contrary of what they ought. Now, granted they are licensed to make so many mistakes without reproach, we shall never succeed in arousing laughter if we insist on attacking them for those deficiencies which we've agreed are all permitted, and not inappropriate to them and not guarded against. Because you have already said that laughter is aroused by what is inappropriate.

LA DUCHESSA: So this is the way in which you speak of women, Signor Ottaviano. And do you, then, complain that they don't love you?

OTTAVIANO: Of that I do not complain. On the contrary, I'm grateful for it, because they do not, by loving me, oblige me to love them; and I am not giving my own opinion, but saying that the Signor Gasparo might put forward such views.

BERNARDO: The ladies would certainly score a great success if they could make their peace with two such formidable enemies as yourself and the Signor Gasparo.

GASPARO: I am no enemy of theirs. On the other hand, you are undoubtedly an enemy to men. Why, if you really believe that women ought not to be attacked on the subject of chastity, then you should impose a rule on them too, that they must not attack men in a direction as shameful to us as incontinence is to them. Consider the case of Boccaccio's Beatrice, who persuades her husband to dress up as herself in order to repel Anichino's advances. She then lies with Anichino and sends him down to beat her husband. You call these female tricks in Boccaccio clever and delightful.

BERNARDO: Gentlemen, my task was to deal only with humour, and I have no intention of going beyond it. To return to the practical jokes played by women, I don't say they do well to deceive their husbands, but I do say that a number of the female deceptions described by Boccaccio are extremely clever and delightful — and in particular the one you yourself have referred to. Beatrice deceived her husband in pursuit of her own pleasure.

GASPARO: On no other grounds can one excuse Beatrice, except that she was in love; and that should rank as an excuse for men, as well as for women.

BERNARDO: It is true that the passions of love provide a good excuse for all shortcomings. Nevertheless, my own opinion is that a gentleman of worth who is in love ought in this as in everything else to be sincere and honest; and I believe that every gentleman in love endures so many labours and vigils, faces so many dangers, sheds so many tears, and employs so many ways and means to please the beloved woman, as he does, not chiefly to obtain her body, but to conquer the fortress of her soul. And undoubtedly, were I myself in love, I would rather have the certain knowledge, without any other satisfaction, that she whom I served loved me in return and gave me her soul, than enjoy her, and have all the rest against her will; for in such a case I would think myself the master of a body that was dead.

GASPARO: I don't deny that the aim, the efforts and the risks accepted by lovers should be directed chiefly towards winning the soul rather than the body of the beloved woman; but I say that these deceptions, which you call betrayals in men and practical jokes in women, are the best means of achieving their purposes for invariably the man who possesses a woman's body is master of her soul as well.

BERNARDO: You are making the most inaccurate of assumptions, for if women always gave their souls to the possessor of their bodies, none would be found who did not love their husbands more than any other person in the world. You are very much in the wrong to be an enemy to women.

GASPARO: Indeed I am not their enemy. But few men of worth are to be found who generally take much notice of women, even if they pretend the contrary now and then — for reasons of their own.

BERNARDO: You are doing an injury not only to women but to all men who hold them in respect. Nevertheless, as I have said, I'd rather not, at the moment, go beyond my assignment of discussing practical jokes, in order to embark on an enterprise as difficult as the defence of women against such a mighty warrior as yourself. Therefore I will make an end of my address, which has possibly gone on much longer than was necessary and has certainly given less pleasure than you expected: and since I observe the ladies remaining so quiet and supporting your slanders so patiently, I shall assume from now on that a part of what the Signor Ottaviano has said is the truth, and that they do not care what hard things are said of them, provided they are not accused of loose living.

CASTIGLIONE: At this point, most of the ladies, at a sign from the Signora Duchessa, rose to their feet and ran laughing towards the Signor Gasparo, as if to rain blows upon him.

LADIES: Now you shall see whether we care about slanders. (etc.)

GASPARO: There you are! Because they're in the wrong, they resort to violence!

LA DUCHESSA: Not at all. You saw Messer Bernardo growing tired after his long address, and started to say such hard things of women in the belief that there was no-one to contradict you; but in order that your mistake shall not go unpunished for long, we'll put a fresher champion into the lists to do combat with you . . . You, Signor Magnifico, have spoken little up to now. You are regarded as the protector of women, and now is the time to prove you have not gained the title falsely.

IL MAGNIFICO: Your Grace, it seems to me that you are doing great honour to your enemy and little to your defender, because up to now the Signor Gasparo has certainly said nothing against women which has not been most excellently countered by Messer Bernardo; and I believe every one of us is aware that it is fitting for the Courtier to hold women in the highest respect, and that he who is discreet and courteous ought never to accuse them of sexual laxity, either seriously or for a joke: so that arguing this obvious fact is almost to raise a doubt concerning matters not in dispute. It does seem to me that the Signor Ottaviano has gone a little too far in calling women the most imperfect of creatures, of little or not value in comparison to men; and because assent is often given to those of great authority, even when they are not speaking the exact truth, the Signor Gasparo has been encouraged by the Signor Ottaviano's remarks to say that wise men take little notice of women. And that is most untrue. On the contrary, I have known few men of worth who do not admire and respect women, whose value — and consequently dignity — I hold to be not a fraction inferior to that of men. Nevertheless, if one had to join in this argument, the woman's cause would be at a great disadvantage: because these gentlemen have created a Courtier so excellent and endowed with so many superhuman qualities, that the merits of women would not be able to rise to them. But if the matter were to be debated under fair conditions, it would be necessary, first of all, for someone as clever and eloquent as the Count Lodovico and Messer Federico to create a Court Lady with all the perfections appropriate to woman, just as they have created the Courtier with all perfections appropriate to man; and then even if he who defended their cause was of no more than average cleverness and eloquence, I think that, as truth would be on his side, he would clearly prove that women are as virtuous as men.

SIGNORA EMILIA: Much more so, in fact. For the word virtue is feminine in our language, and vice is masculine.

GASPARO: Frigio! What have you to say about all that? I am sorry for the Signor Magnifico, who has been inveigled by the promises and flattery of the Signora Emilia into saying things that I, as a member of his staff, am ashamed of.

SIGNORA EMILIA: You'll certainly be ashamed on your own account as well, when you see the Signor Gasparo forced to admit that you're both in the wrong — and offering the apology which we won't be willing to accept.

LA DUCHESSA: As it is now very late, I wish to postpone the discussion until tomorrow, the more so because it seems right to accept the Signor Magnifico's advice which is — before we embark on this argument — to create a Court Lady with every perfection, just as these gentlemen have created a faultless Courtier.

SIGNORA EMILIA: Madam, may God grant that we don't happen to lay this task on someone in league with the Signor Gasparo, someone who will create a Court Lady for us that knows nothing, except how to sew and cook!

FRIGIO: That is indeed her proper department.

La Duchessa: I am content to pin my faith on the Signor Magnifico. I am confident that his talent and discrimination will enable him to picture the highest perfection one could ask for in a woman, and will command the necessary words to express it; and so we shall have something to oppose to the Signor Gasparo's false calumnies.

Il Magnifico: Your Grace, I am not sure how well advised you are in laying on me an enterprise of such importance; for the truth is, I do not feel myself equal to it; and I do not resemble the Conte and Messer Federico, who have created by their eloquence a Courtier who never existed — and perhaps never could. Still, if it is your pleasure that I should shoulder this burden, let it at least be under the same conditions as these other gentlemen, which are that anyone may contradict me when he sees fit; for I shall regard this, not as contradiction, but assistance; and perhaps the correcting of my mistakes will reveal that perfection of the Court Lady which we seek.

La Duchessa: I hope your discussion will be of the kind that admits little contradiction. Therefore concentrate your thoughts on this question only, and create for us such a Lady that these our adversaries will blush to say that she is not of equal worth to the Courtier, of whom Messer Federico should say no more, since he has endowed him far too well for one who is to stand comparison with a woman.

Frigio: Your Grace, there remains little or nothing more for me to say on the subject of the Courtier, and what I had prepared has been allowed, by Messer Bernardo's examples of humour, to escape my memory.

La Duchessa: If this is the case, we shall, by assembling early tomorrow, have leisure to satisfy ourselves on both these questions.

Castiglione: At these words they all rose to their feet, respectfully took their leave of the Signora Duchessa, and dispersed to their own rooms . . . When the company had assembled on the following day, at the accustomed time and place, and taken their places in silence, everyone turned his eyes towards Messer Federico and the Magnifico Giuliano, wondering which of them would begin the discussion. When they had been silent for a time, the Signora Duchessa spoke . . .

LA DUCHESSA: Signor Magnifico, everyone wishes to view this Court Lady of yours — in suitable apparel; and if you do not exhibit her in such a way that all her charms are visible, we shall assume that you are jealous of them.

IL MAGNIFICO: Your Grace, if I considered her beautiful, I would exhibit her in that state in which Paris chose to view the three goddesses, without further embellishment; but unless these ladies lend me their expert assistance in dressing her, I fear that not only the Signor Gasparo and Messer Ottaviano, but all these other gentlemen, will have just cause to speak badly of her. And therefore, while she still has some reputation for beauty, perhaps it would be better to keep her veiled, and see what Messer Federico has to say about the Courtier, who no doubt is much more handsome than my Court Lady can hope to be.

FRIGIO: What I have in mind is not so closely related to the Courtier that it cannot be omitted without any harm being done; on the contrary, it stands apart from anything we have so far discussed.

LA DUCHESSA: May one ask what it is?

FRIGIO: I had intended, as far as possible, to describe what led to the founding of those Companies and Orders of knighthood by great princes under various insignias — for example: that of Saint Michael in the French royal family, that of the Garter in England, of the Golden Fleece in Burgundy . . . I had also intended, if time allowed, to consider the customs of oriental as well as Christian courts, in particular that of the King of Persia. For I understand from merchants who have spent a long time in the country, that the noblemen there are very courageous and observe customs of great refinement, both among themselves and in the service of women. But this is certainly not a convenient time to embark on such a discussion for there are other matters of much greater urgency and more to the purpose than that.

GASPARO: On the contrary, that and many other matters are more to the purpose than the formation of this Court

Lady. It's understood that the same rules as were laid down for the Courtier apply also to her, for she should adapt herself to the place and the occasion and she should observe, in so far as her idiocy permits her, all those other usages we have so long discussed — exactly as the Courtier does. And therefore, instead of this, it might perhaps have been in order to instruct us in some of the details of personal attendance on a Prince, for the Courtier ought certainly to know them and to perform them elegantly. Or why not, indeed, speak of the methods one should adopt in physical exercises: riding, handling, weapons, wrestling?

LA DUCHESSA: Princes do not employ so excellent a Courtier as this in personal attendance. As for physical exercises, and strength and agility, Pietro Monte is here to instruct you, when he finds it convenient . . . But here and now the Magnifico has no other theme than this Court Lady, of whom it seems to me you are already beginning to be afraid and therefore want us to change the subject.

FRIGIO: It certainly is ill-timed and off the subject to talk about women now, when urgent things remains to be said of the Courtier. One should not confuse one theme with another.

SIGNOR GONZAGA: You are greatly mistaken, because just as no court, no matter how powerful, can have adornment or splendour or gaiety without women; and no Courtier can be elegant, charming and adventurous, or ever perform a gracious deed of chivalry, unless he be set in motion by experience of women, by the love of women and the pleasure it affords; so it follows that discussion of the Courtier is always incomplete unless women intervene and contribute the grace with which they perfect and adorn courtly behaviour.

OTTAVIANO: There you have a sample of food which produces insanity when eaten by man. [*Laughter*]

IL MAGNIFICO: Your Grace . . .

LA DUCHESSA: Signor Magnifico?

Il Magnifico: Your Grace, in deference to your wishes, I will say what I have in mind, though in the greatest apprehension that it will prove insufficient; and it would certainly be a much easier task to create a lady fit to be Queen of the World, than a perfect Lady of the Court. For of the latter I do not know where to take an example; whereas of the Queen I should not have to look very far; I would need only to bring into focus the divine attributes of a lady I actually know, and as I held them in contemplation, to concentrate all my thoughts on describing clearly in words what many are aware of through their eyes; and were I able to do no more, I would, simply by naming her, have discharged my obligation.

LA DUCHESSA: Do not digress, Signor Magnifico, but pay attention to the orders given you and create the Court Lady, so that this excessively noble person may have someone worthy of waiting on her.

IL MAGNIFICO: Your Grace, to show that your commands can steel me to attempt even that which is beyond my power, I shall describe this excellent Lady as I would wish her to be; and when I have created her according to my own taste, I will, as I may have no other, follow Pygmalion's example and take her for myself. Although the Signor Gasparo has said that the same rules as were laid down for the Courtier apply also to the Lady, I hold a different opinion. For although some qualities are as necessary to the man as to the woman and are common to both, there are others more suited to the woman than to the man, and others, again, suitable to the man, which must yet be entirely foreign to her. I say the same of physical exercises. But above all, it seems to me that in her attitude, her manners, words, gestures and bearing, the woman is bound to be very different. Because, just as it is fitting for him to display a certain type of reliable and inflexible virility, so it is becoming in the woman to have a yielding and delicate tenderness, moulding her every movement in such a way that — whether she be in motion or at rest or merely talking — it always proclaims her as female, with no resemblance whatever to a man . . . All the same, I agree with the Signor Gasparo that many spiritual virtues are as requisite in her as in the man: nobility, avoidance of affectation, an inborn elegance in every undertaking: she should be good-mannered, clever, prudent — not proud, not envious, not slanderous, not vain, not quarrelsome, not clumsy; she should know how to gain and keep the favour of her signora and of everyone else. I am firmly of the opinion that personal beauty is more necessary to her than to the Courtier, for a great deal is lacking in the woman who lacks that. She must also be discreet, and more careful to avoid anything which might stir up scandal, and so conduct herself that not only does she avoid the smear of guilt, but even the suspicion of it — because fewer means of defence against false aspersions are open to a woman . . . Since the Conte Ludovico has explained in such great detail the Courtier's chief profession — arms, according to him — I feel it is in order that I should go on to say what, in my opinion, that of the Court Lady ought to be. And when I have done so I'll consider that I have discharged the major part of my obligation . . . Leaving aside, then, those spiritual virtues she should possess in common with the Courtier — and similarly those appropriate to all women, such as goodness and discretion, the ability to take care of her husband's resources, her home and her children, and all the accomplishments required of a married woman with a family; in addition to this, I say that, to the lady whose life is passed in Courts, there is, to my mind, appropriate above all other things a kind of *agreeable affability*. It renders her capable of sustaining polite conversation with every type of man, of giving pleasure without loss of self-respect, of adapting herself to the time, the place, the rank of the person concerned; it is accompanied by manners of tranquil modesty, and — together with that self-respect which must always be at the root of all her actions — an alert liveliness of spirit, which shows how far she is from any coarseness . . . But even where she is involved in company and conversation of rather a lascivious tone, this lady should not be so chary of her reputation for virtue and self-respect, so prudish and anxious to show her loathing, as to rise and walk out. You see, it could well be thought that she was acting so extreme an austerity, in order to hide some tendency she was afraid might be discovered in herself; and such provincial manners are invariably repulsive. She ought still less, in the hope of appearing winsome and emancipated, to indulge in bad language or affect a lax and unrestrained familiarity. And similarly, she must avoid a mistake I have seen many fall into — namely speaking ill of other women and listening eagerly to those who slander them. Women who spend their time prying into the bad behaviour of others, and reporting it with such exactitude and delight, give the impression of being motivated by envy; and hence it arises that men, although they appear glad to listen, more often than not have a bad opinion of the speaker and interpret her conduct as an invitation to make advances. Whereas, poise, tempered by wisdom and kindness, acts as a shield against the insolence and bestility of the presumptuous . . . The Court Lady should have a wide general knowledge, without being so inept as to claim to know what in fact she does not. Let her seek to be honoured for what she does know and, as we have said, avoid in everything *affectation*. On these lines she will be adorned with good manners, and those physical exercises proper to a woman she will perform with supreme elegance, and her conversation will be plentiful, brimming with prudence, self-respect and charm; and so she will be not only loved, but revered by all the world, and worthy, perhaps — of parity with this grand Courtier. [*Pause*]

GASPARO: Signor Magnifico, you have indeed generously adorned this Lady and given her excellent attainments; nevertheless, it seems to me that you have restricted yourself very much to generalities and named in her a number of qualities so great that I believe any attempt to enlarge on them would put you to shame. For example, I would like you to inform us rather more exactly of the physical exercises proper to a Lady of the Court. [*Magnifico laughs*]

IL MAGNIFICO: Signor Gasparo, you simply cannot refrain from showing ill-will towards the ladies; but I did indeed think I had said enough, especially before such listeners as these; for I am certain no-one here is ignorant of the fact that, where physical exercises are concerned, it is unseemly for a woman to bear arms, ride, play tennis or wrestle.

BERNARDO: Among the ancients it was customary for men to wrestle with women in the nude, but we have discontinued that admirable usage, along with many others.

SIGNOR GONZAGA: And in my time, I myself have seen women play tennis, handle weapons, ride, go hunting, and perform almost all the exercises known to a cavalier.

IL MAGNIFICO: Since I am allowed to create this Lady according to my own taste, I had rather she abstained from such rough and vigorous manly exercises; and even when dancing I would prefer not to see her engage in excessively forceful and athletic movements. As for music, how disastrous it would be to see a woman playing drums, pipes, trumpets or other instruments of the kind; and this because their crudity conceals and detracts from that gentle delicacy which so adorns a woman's every action. But because it is permitted, in fact obligatory, for women to pay more attention to personal beauty than is the case with men, and as there are different types of beauty, this Lady should have enough discrimination to know which are the garments to enhance her grace. If she knows herself to have a gay and pretty kind of beauty, she ought to assist it with movements, words and garments all tending towards gaiety; just as another, conscious of being gentle and solemn in demeanour, should link it with apparel of the same type, so as to emphasise what nature has given her. Similarly, if she is a little stouter or thinner, darker or fairer than is normal, she should dissimulate the fact as much as possible with the help of her attire; and while keeping herself neat and well-groomed, let her always appear to take no thought or pains about it . . . To sum up, I require this Lady to know something of literature, music and painting, and to be able to dance and organise celebrations. And although continence, magnanimity, temperance, strength of mind, prudence and the other virtues seem irrelevant to entertainment, I want her adorned with them all: not so much for entertainment — although in that, too, they can be of use — as to render her virtuous; and in order that these virtues make her such that she is worthy of esteem, and that everything she undertakes may be composed of them.

GASPARO: Since you bestow on women learning, continence, magnanimity and temperance, I marvel that you would not also have them govern cities as well, make laws and command armies — while the men are occupied with cooking or needlework. [*Magnifico laughs*]

IL MAGNIFICO: Perhaps that might not be a bad idea, after all! Are you not aware that Plato — who was not, indeed, any too friendly towards women — awards them the custody of cities while giving all the other military responsibilities to men? Don't you think many are to be found who would control cities and armies as well as men do? But I have not awarded them those positions, because I am creating a Court Lady, not a Queen. I know quite well you want to repeat, by implication, those untrue slanders which the Signor Ottaviano uttered yesterday against women.

GASPARO: I do not want to repeat anything already said; but your intention is to lead me into saying something defamatory of these ladies in our company, so as to make them my enemies; just as you would like to ingratiate yourself with them by insincere flattery. However, their discretion is so greatly superior to that of others of their sex, that they value the truth, even when it is not very much in their favour, above unmerited praise. They will admit that you have recounted miracles and given the Court Lady absurdly impossible attributes, along with so many virtues that Socrates, Cato, and all the philosophers in history would be left in the shade. You might well have been content with giving her every conceivable social accomplishment; but endowing her with the sum of worldly knowledge, and those virtues which are so rarely found in men, even in centuries gone by, is a thing one cannot endure and, in fact, scarcely listen to . . . Not that I wish to affirm that women are imperfect creatures and consequently of less dignity than men for the quality of the ladies here present would be enough to prove me a liar. What I do say is that the wisest of men have written to the effect that nature, whose aim and object is always to create things of the greatest perfection, would produce only men, if that were possible; and when a woman is born, it is by an oversight or mistake, contrary to nature's intention — just as one sees people born blind, lame, or with some other defect, and trees bearing fruit which never ripens. Nevertheless, as the defects in women are the fault of nature, which has made them so, we ought not to hate them on that account, or fail to hold them in as much respect as is fitting. But to esteem them beyond what they are seems to me a manifest error.

IL MAGNIFICO: I think you have put forward a most heartless explanation of the imperfections of women, and although it may not be fitting to discuss finer points of philosophy, I am ready to answer in your own terms.

GASPARO: I had rather we did not discuss such fine points, for these ladies will not understand us. [*Laughter and protests*]

Other Titles from
FORESTBOOKS

International Poetry Series

THE NAKED MACHINE Selected poems of Matthías Johannessen.
Translated from the *Icelandic* by Marshall Brement.
(Forest/Almenna bokáfélagid)
0 948259 44 2 cloth £7.95 0 948259 43 4 paper £5.95 96pages Illustrated

ON THE CUTTING EDGE Selected poems of Justo Jorge Padrón.
Translated from the *Spanish* by Louis Bourne.
0 948259 42 6 paper £8.95 176 pages

ROOM WITHOUT WALLS Selected poems of Bo Carpelan.
Translated from the *Swedish* by Anne Born.
0 948259 08 6 paper £7.95 144 pages. Illustrated

CALL YOURSELF ALIVE? The love poems of Nina Cassian.
Translated from the *Romanian* by Andrea Deletant and
Brenda Walker. Introduction by Fleur Adcock.
0 948259 38 8 paper £6.95. 96 pages. Illustrated

A VANISHING EMPTINESS Selected poems of Willem M. Roggeman.
Edited by Yann Lovelock. Translated from the *Dutch*.
0 948259 51 5 paper £7.95 112 pages. Illustrated

PORTRAIT OF THE ARTIST AS AN ABOMINABLE SNOWMAN
Selected poems of Gabriel Rosenstock translated from the
Irish by Michael Hartnett. New Poems translated by Jason Sommer.
0 948259 56 6 paper £7.95 112 pages Dual text

LAND AND PEACE Selected poems of Desmond Egan.
Translated *into Irish* by Michael Hartnett, Gabriel Rosenstock,
Douglas Sealey and Tomas MacSiomoin. Dual text.
0 948259 64 7 paper £7.95 112 pages

THE EYE IN THE MIRROR Selected poems of Takis Varvitsiotis.
Translated from the *Greek* by Kimon Friar. (Forest/Paratiritis)
0 948259 59 0 paper £8.95 160 pages

THE WORLD AS IF Selected poems of Uffe Harder.
Translated from the *Danish* by John F. Deane and Uffe Harder.
(Dedalus/Forest)
0 948259 76 0 paper £4.95   80 pages

SPRING TIDE Selected poems of Pia Tafdrup.
Translated from the *Danish* by Anne Born.
0 948259 55 8 paper £7.95   96 pages

SNOW AND SUMMERS Selected poems of Solveig von Schoultz.
Translated from *Finland/Swedish* by Anne Born.
Introduction by Bo Carpelan. Arts Council funded.
0 948259 52 3 paper £7.95   112 pages

FOOTPRINTS OF THE WIND Selected poems of Mateja Matevski.
Translated from the *Macedonian* by Ewald Osers.
Introduction by Robin Skelton. Arts Council funded.
0 948259 41 8 paper £6.95   96 pages. Illustrated

ARIADNE'S THREAD An anthology of contemporary Polish women poets. Translated from the *Polish* by Susan Bassnett and Piotr Kuhiwczak. UNESCO collection of representative works.
0 948259 45 0 paper £6.95   96 pages

POETS OF BULGARIA An anthology of contemporary Bulgarian poets.
Edited by William Meredith. Introduction by Alan Brownjohn.
0 948259 39 6 paper £6.95   112 pages

FIRES OF THE SUNFLOWER Selected poems by Ivan Davidkov.
Translated from the *Bulgarian* by Ewald Osers.
0 948259 48 5 paper £6.95   96 pages.   Illustrated

STOLEN FIRE Selected poems by Lyubomir Levchev.
Translated from the *Bulgarian* by Ewald Osers.
Introduction by John Balaban.
UNESCO collection of representative works.
0 948259 04 3 paper £6.95   112 pages.   Illustrated

AN ANTHOLOGY OF CONTEMPORARY ROMANIAN POETRY
Translated by Andrea Deletant and Brenda Walker.
0 9509487 4 8 paper £6.95   112 pages.

GATES OF THE MOMENT Selected poems of Ion Stoica.
Translated from the *Romanian* by Brenda Walker and Andrea Deletant. Dual text with cassette.
0 9509487 0 5 paper £6.95   126 pages   Cassette £3.50 plus VAT

THE ROAD TO FREEDOM Poems and Prose Poems by Geo Milev
Translated from the *Bulgarian* by Ewald Osers.
UNESCO collection of representative works.
0 948259 40 X paper £6.95 96 pages Illustrated

IN CELEBRATION OF MIHAI EMINESCU Selected poems and extracts translated from the *Romanian* by Brenda Walker and Horia Florian Popescu. Illustrated by Sabin Balaşa.
0 948259 62 0 cloth Limited edition £20 176 pages

THROUGH THE NEEDLE'S EYE Selected poems of Ion Milos.
Translated from the *Romanian* by Brenda Walker and Ion Milos.
0 948259 61 2 paper £6.95 96 pages. Illustrated

JOUSTS OF APHRODITE Poems collected from the Greek Anthology Book V
Translated from the *Greek* into modern English by Michael Kelly.
0 948259 05 1 cloth £6.95 0 948259 34 5 paper £4.95 96 pages

FISH-RINGS ON WATER Selected poems by Katherine Gallagher, the *Australian* poet. Introduced by Peter Porter.
0 948259 75 2 paper £6.95 96 pages Illustrated

PIED POETS An anthology of Romanian Transylvanian and Danube poets writing in German. Translated from the *German* by Robert Elsie.
Dual text English/German. Arts Council funded
0 948259 77 9 paper £10.95 192 pages

BEFORE WE WERE STRANGERS Poems by the *American* poet Nadya Aisenberg.
Introduced by Sylvia Kantaris.
0 948259 81 7 paper £6.95 96 pages

WASTELANDS OF FIRE Poems by Ku Sang.
Translated from the *Korean* by Anthony Teague.
0 948259 82 5 paper £7.95 144 pages

CLOSED CIRCUIT by Shadab Vajdi.
Translated from the *Persian* by Lotfali Kohonji and introduced by Peter Avery.
0 948259 78 7 paper £6.95 96 pages

STEP HUMAN INTO THIS WORLD Poems by Olaf Munzberg.
Translated from the *German* by Mitch Cohen.
0 948259 53 1 paper £6.95 96 pages

ENCHANTING BEASTS An anthology of Finnish women poets.
Translated from the *Finnish* and the *Swedish* by Kirsti Simonsuuri.
0 948259 68 X paper £8.95 160 pages

SILENT VOICES An anthology of contemporary Romanian women poets. Translated by Andrea Deletant and Brenda Walker.
0 948259 03 5 paper £8.95 172 pages

EXILE ON A PEPPERCORN Selected poems of Mircea Dinescu.
Translated from the *Romanian* by Andrea Deletant and Brenda Walker.
0 948259 00 0 paper £7.95 96 pages. Illustrated

LET'S TALK ABOUT THE WEATHER Selected poems of Marin Sorescu
Translated from the *Romanian* by Andrea Deletant and Brenda Walker.
0 9509487 8 0 paper £6.95 96 pages

International Drama Series

THE THIRST OF THE SALT MOUNTAIN Three plays by Marin Sorescu (Jonah, The Verger, and the Matrix) Translated from the *Romanian* by Andrea Deletant and Brenda Walker.
0 9509487 5 6 paper £7.95 124 pages. Illustrated

VLAD DRACULA THE IMPALER A play by Marin Sorescu
Translated from the *Romanian* by Dennis Deletant.
0 948259 07 8 paper £6.95 112 pages. Illustrated

International Short Story Series

RUNNING TO THE SHROUDS Six sea stories of Konstantin Stanyukovich.
Translated from the *Russian* by Neil Parsons.
0 948259 06 X paper £6.95 112 pages.

HEARTWORK Stories of Solveig von Schoultz.
Translated from *Finland/Swedish* by Marlaine Delargy and Joan Tate. Introduction by Bo Carpelan.
0 948259 50 7 paper £7.95 144 pages

THICKHEAD AND OTHER STORIES by Haldun Taner.
Translated from the *Turkish* by Geoffrey Lewis.
UNESCO collection of representative works.
0 948259 58 2 paper £8.95 176 pages

YOUTH WITHOUT YOUTH and other Novellas by Mircea Eliade.
Edited and with an introduction by Matei Calinescu.
Translated from the *Romanian* by MacLinscott Ricketts.
0 948259 74 4 paper £12.95 328 pages

A WOMAN'S HEART Stories by Jordan Yovkov.
Translated from the *Bulgarian* by John Burnip.
0 948259 54 X paper £9.95 208 pages

THE SEER AND OTHER STORIES by Jonas Lie.
Translated from the *Norwegian* by Brian Morton and Richard Trevor.
0 948259 65 5 paper £9.95 208 pages

THE TALISMAN Stories and poems by Ganga Prasad Vimal.
Edited by Wendy Wright. G.L.A. funded.
0 948259 57 4 paper £9.95 208 pages Dual text English/Hindi.

PREPARATIONS FOR FLIGHT and other Swedish stories.
Translated from the *Swedish* by Robin Fulton.
0 948259 66 3 paper £8.95 176 pages.